AFFECTION

ECLECTIC POETRY

NAMAYLIN

Contents

Chapter1

Wind breeze

I can only feel your pleasant presence

Rain drops tells our story beyond the sky

Each drops of wonders and love that made life worthy

You're the reason that I started to love myself

Only you

My eyes are filled with tears of love

Which turns into a shiny white pearl

When you see me through your glazed twinkling bright eye

The past gets paused and the present light up

You are perfect, the world deserves you

You are the sunshine You are the star ,

Helped me fondly to be fearless of the night.

Chapter2

Oh, this sea is calling me
The waves made by an oar
You came to me like a wave
The first drop of rain
Felt so warm
I was soaked when it touched me
The cloud has wandered
And melted into me
Hey breeze please flow on this branch
Rain falls on this leaf
Slowly to this shore
You became my shelter
Like a tree branch
You opened like an umbrella to me.

Chapter3

•3•

Sky was welcoming a new day
I persisted because
I just knew
A wait for a real love
Is worth waiting
Blessing descended in the twilight
To hold me tight
And see me through your eyes
To love my eyes
Stay with me up till
Oceans become clam and run dry
Stay with me .
A feeling of completeness
Only you
With you I am everything.

Chapter4

You are the hmm of my music
I never knew from where to
Begin the musical note
Listen this song
It's my feelings
I have always wanted to tell you.
I whim you to listen
Hold your hands
Make you feel loved
I am certain
I will love you forever
I can give you instances
My love will be always here for you
Right here.

Chapter5

I can't see, how I can go on living

Away from you

Let not the light see

Let not the flowers listen

Let not the spring embrace

I am going to say ,hear it

I adore you to depths

Beyond the eyes can see

We are in each other all along

You embrace me

You bring rainbows

In my life.

Chapter6

Love likes to hide itself
Love can lose itself
Love is curious
It can ring in at
Edge of the sea shore
Edge of a mountain
Edge of a street
Edge of a fountain
Where love poem is written
With dreamy eyes
Love is dreamy
Love will find you in

Its own way.

Chapter7

Your smile is heaven
Makes hundreds to amend
Full of enrichment
Your eyes tell me all about you.
World feels totally diverse when I am with you Without you the
world is not perfect enough for me
Our friendship should last for millions of year.
You are my living paradise
You filled my grey life into a colourful one
You are my guardian angel…

Chapter8

I asked you what makes you delighted

You told Me

You cannot envision this moment

You always gave me the best out of you

I realized you are the person

Always embrace me

Guided and turned my regrets and mistakes

Into best life lessons

I want to give the same love you gave me

Flowers blooms with your mist presence

Sun is for the day and moon is for the night

but you are my forever.

You are the key to open the door

To my future.

Chapter9

From special
To somebody very special one
My best one forever
I open my eyes and look at your smiling face
Every morning
My day begins with you and ends with you
Your smiley face wishes good luck.
Always accompany me in my happiness and sorrows
You are the one who have
Seen my happiest and saddest days
I have ever had.
Your hug always comforts and consoles me
My universal happiness it's you
You give me more energy to live on
My companion
Only person who doesn't let me down
My Mom

Chapter10

City with no laughter
Looking for new shores
The heart without desire
Far from the eyes
Eyelid lights lamps
While thinking about you
The night glows brighter
A thousand stars shines
You're smile is like first snowfall
My desire lights up like
The beautiful bright sky
Just like you.

Chapter11

Perhaps I had been alone

If perhaps

I must have given up in myself and lost in the sea, The moment you

appeared in front of me

You were the one I was looking for

It felt as we had met in dreams

My heart fluttered just when our eyes meet

Within a split for second my world

Turned upside down

If stars could hear my prayers

Even for a day

I would wish , my heart to get closer to yours.

Chapter12

No amount of words
could properly describe
what I feel
every poem or quote I write is incomplete
because I can't
put myself into it nowadays
I'll always want
to make understand myself
but the distance reaches deeper
than poetry ever could...

Chapter13

Someday are so hard.

Life feels hopeless

Just wanted to disappear from this world.

Nasty people around ,

Mind full of negatives

Crying in the darkness

Under the blanket ... hoping that one day Everything will be good .

What to do ,what to do.

Always putting a fake smile

Smiling in front of my loved once.

Just to make them happy.

But deep down I am dyeing

Hope one day ,stars will show me the light from this darkness.

Chapter14

I can promise

I will aways be here for you

Always here to listen

Always here to hold your hands

Always here and make you

Feel loved

Always dream with you

Always cheer for you

I love you and will love you

Till blue in the face

Always with you

World without end.

Where it belongs ,In your eyes

Your soul and between our holding hands Somewhere only we know

Love you endlessly.

Chapter15

Every time I see you
The sun was shining in the sky
There isn't a cloud in sight
My heart drives me crazy
It leaves me feeling seasick
Wind blowing, wind blowing
I would wish for my heart to
Get close to you
Emotion I have for you
It will never change.
Your presence made the clouds
The sky was completely mesmerizing
Every moment of my life has become priceless
I have a good luck always with me
It's you.

Chapter16

Our tale never ends

You are that one star fell into my life

A story tale remains eternal

No matter how many times the story is apprehend Remains the same

endlessly

Perhaps I had no idea my heart harmonizes to you

I do not have a reason to justify

Everything between us does not need an answer Our love remnant

the same.

We will reach each other as two rays of moon One day.

My heart beat encore

Because

You are my heartbeat .

Chapter17

The first drop of rain drop came down

My heart was beautiful soaked with sweetness butterflies searching for

nectar

life seems to be sweet and euphoric

nectar made me divine

you are the only one I have been waiting

want to spend all my life with you

All my life

Life is flower for which ,love is the nectar

my life is a flower and you are the nectar

love is the honey for the flower

you're the only one for me

your sweetness makes me bloom

you are the only sunshine all the time in my life

my love always belongs to you

you are the only one I have been waiting

only one all this time

in my life, my love.

Chapter18

Beauty is how you feel inward
The Sparkle in your eyes
reflects and tell who you are
live life deliberately
and use the time wisely
perceive your passion
that's the beauty you need.
when you go deep you will get know your true self beautiful deep
down to soul,
It creates a magical light in the heart
be clam and still like an ocean
bloom like a flower
beautiful and unique
be unique.

Chapter19

When things were arduous
I was drained of living
When aught was going away
Inner feeling throbs my heart saying
I was not earnest to myself,
In the edge of falling
Wishing luminary to hold my hand
Take my whole life
Because I can't help myself
Never asked for de trop.
I look and search
Stay up at night to meet
The old me
I have vicissitude a lot,
Hope it will reanimate fast
I can meet my old self.

Chapter20

The moon light hits your shadow
I see your smile
I see you in my dreams
When you smile your eyes shines like a
meteor shower
My heart and earth share the same rule
It starts with love and ends with you
You don't know yet
You were my beloved one
You're my everything, my everything
I will give you my everything,
all the joy and happiness
My heart gazed the movement I met you.
You are my destiny.

Chapter21

When I am happy stay with me

Stay with me in all my moments

I want to sing a song

This unbelievable feeling

Feels like a castle in the air

I don't know where I belong,

I don't know why I smile looking your eyes.,

I smile without a reason

I fell in love with you.

Chapter22

Astray cloudy days,
Dreams about touching
feeling the cloud.
Day by Day
Clouds look dark and ominous
Just floating alone
In the empty sky
Dark cloud hover over our lives
The rainbows turning into black
Life is not easy not perfect.
The fog begins to disappear
Gentle as ever ,far way
Like the moon behind the cloud
Like a rainbow afraid to come out.
Have so much depths
Lingering in the sky
Clouds look dark and ominous...
Day by Day.

Chapter23

My feelings for you are flourishing deeper and deeper each day.

I forgot about myself

I know it's not perfect ,

but I still can't control myself

Because you are my first love ,

The one who made me to visualize about myself. You are the star that

I can't even reach out .,

When you shine up there ,

Make my heart warm

You're my happiness , you're my everything ,

I just hope to see you once in my life,

you're beautiful smile,

once in my life

My first and last thought is only about you,

I love you ;I want you

But I can't you deserve the

World That isn't just me

I will pray for you

That one day you will find your world

That I know I never can,

Because this is not our story.

Chapter24

I asked you what makes you happy
You told me
You just can't realize this moment
You always gave me the best of you
This time I'll give back the love to you
Only because of you I realized that
I was able to love my life so much
You always embrace me
You turned my regrets and mistake
s into best life lessons
I want to give out a lot of love to you
When I talk to you the flowers bloom again The night turns into day
We can share our good times and bad times with each other forever
You gave me the key to open the door to my future I realized that
I was able to love my life so much only because of you .
You always embrace me...

Chapter25

There is no limit in this sky
To express my feelings towards you
My life was colourless
you filled colour
A colour that emanating mysterious wonders
You are
Like the mist on an early spring morning over the bushes,
The sun light reflects and the mist turns just purplish like you ,
When u smile
The clouds welcome's the most precious ray in the rainbow ,
The fast few seconds of a sunset,
It's the beautiful view we get to see
And I want to see it with you , filling more purplish happiness to it.,
In music purple would be soft but
A strong melody like you,
A melody that takes me to another universe
The sun was shining in the sky
There isn't a cloud in sight
Your presence made the clouds filled with
joy and happiness, prosperity like purple ,
The sky was completely mesmerizing with purple light,
You're my happiness ,my everything
Every moment of my life has become priceless
I have a good luck always with me
It's you, my purple

End